INSTRUMENTS in MUSIC

RELIGIOUS MUSIC

Roger Thomas

Heinemann Library
Des Plaines, Illinois

Designed by Susan Clarke
Printed in Hong Kong

02 01 00 99 98
10 9 8 7 6 5 4 3 2 1

Library of Congress Cataloging-in-Publication Data

Thomas, Roger, 1956-
　　　Religious music / Roger Thomas.
　　　　　p.　cm. — (Instruments in music)
　　　Includes bibliographical references and index.
　　　Summary: Introduces the role of musical instruments in Christian
and gospel choirs, Tibetan and Japanese temples, Jewish and Hindu
ceremonies, and use by concert, theater, and rock groups.
　　　ISBN 1-57572-644-0 (lib. bdg.)
　　　1. Musical instruments—Religious aspects—Juvenile literature.
2. Sacred vocal music—History and criticism—Juvenile literature.
[1. Musical instruments—Religious aspects. 2. Sacred songs.]
I. Title.　II. Series.
ML460.T424　1998
784.17—dc21
　　　　　　　　　　　　　　　　　　　　　　　　　　97-49504
　　　　　　　　　　　　　　　　　　　　　　　　　　CIP
　　　　　　　　　　　　　　　　　　　　　　　　　　AC　MN

Acknowledgements
The Publishers would like to thank the following for permission to reproduce photographs:
Andes Press Agency, pp.4, 6, 8, 9, 19 (Carlos Reyes-Manzo); Circa Photo Library, p.13; Trevor Clifford, p.17 top left,
top center, bottom left, p.27 left, top left, top right, right (John Myatt Brass and Woodwind), p.17 top right and
bottom right, p.27 center bottom (Parker Brass); Corbis-Bettman, p.26; Hutchison Library, p.23, p.22 (Sarah
Errington); Mary Evans Picture Library, p.15; Panos Pictures, pp.20, 21 (Peter Barker); Redferns, pp.14, 28; Reg
Wilson, p.29; Trip, pp.10, 18 (D. Butcher), p.11 (J. Okwesa); Zefa, pp.5, 7, 12, 16, 25, p.24 (J. Schorken).

Cover photograph:

Our thanks to Betty Root for her comments in the preparation of this book.

Every effort has been made to contact copyright holders of any material reproduced in this book. Any omissions will
be rectified in subsequent printings if notice is given to the Publisher.

Any words appearing in bold, **like this,** are explained in the Glossary.

CONTENTS

INTRODUCTION

Music is very important in most religions. This book tells you about some of the different musical instruments which are used in services and other kinds of worship in religions across the world. It is also about ways of singing in worship, because many more people join in worship by singing than playing instruments.

The voice is the most important "instrument" in religious music.

This Jewish rabbi is playing a traditional horn called a shofar.

You will probably recognize some of the instruments and singing styles in this book, as well as the places where they are used. Some of them will be new to you. But they are all used to help people worship in different religions around the world.

THE CHRISTIAN CHOIR AND CONGREGATION

There is often a choir in a Christian church. A choir is a group of singers who help the congregation to sing the hymns and psalms. They also sing on their own.

Singing is an important part of Christian worship.

The people who sing in the church choir are called choristers.

The singers in the choir will be divided up according to whether their voices are high or low. The choir will often include children because they can sing higher **notes** than adults. The congregation are the people who come to worship in the church. They enjoy singing together with the choir.

GREGORIAN CHANT

Gregorian **chant** is a very old way of singing used by the Roman Catholic Church. It uses only a small number of **notes** and the singers all sing the same notes. It is often sung by people in **religious orders**.

Gregorian chanting often takes place in monastery chapels like this one.

The rhythm in Gregorian Chant is very simple.

Gregorian chant is very simple and gentle because the singers believe this shows respect for God. Many people in the busy world of today like listening to Gregorian chant because it is so peaceful.

THE GOSPEL CHOIR

The best-known kind of Gospel music is the kind sung by choirs in Pentecostal churches in the United States. It is very exciting music which shows the joy of worshipping God. It has lively tunes and strong **rhythms**.

There are often many singers in a Gospel choir.

Gospel music often has folk and blues influences.

Gospel singers often clap their hands and play **percussion** instruments while they sing. In churches a pianist or organist will usually play while the choir sings. Gospel music is also performed in concert halls.

JEWISH MUSIC

A Jewish place of worship is called a synagogue. There will often be a choir who will sing **sacred texts** and songs. An especially gifted singer will often sing a **solo** part in the music. This person is called a cantor.

This cantor has on traditional religious clothing.

This choir is singing in a Jewish synagogue.

There is a very old **tradition** of singing in the Jewish religion. There are special kinds of singing for different ceremonies and for certain special occasions in a person's life.

THE ORGAN AND HARMONIUM

The organ is an instrument often found in churches. It is played using sets of **keyboards** and **pedals**. Its sound comes from big pipes. Air is pushed into the pipes by **bellows**. Today the bellows are powered by electricity, but years ago they had to be pumped by hand. The organ has a loud, powerful sound.

This organist is playing a typical organ.

The harmonium is a smaller type of organ.

The harmonium, or reed organ, is a small organ which uses metal **reeds** instead of pipes to make sounds. Air is pushed through the reeds by bellows. It is not often used today. Because it was small, it was often taken by Christian **missionaries** to faraway countries to use when people sang hymns.

THE SALVATION ARMY

The Salvation Army is a worldwide Christian organization. It encourages Christian beliefs and helps people in need. The Salvation Army has bands which play Christian music in public places. They often use **brass** and **woodwind** instruments.

This is a typical Salvation Army Band.

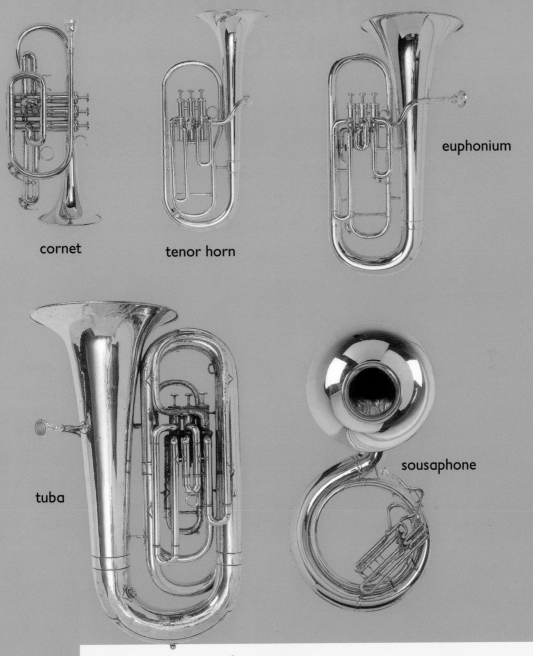

cornet

tenor horn

euphonium

tuba

sousaphone

You might see these instruments in a Salvation Army band.

You will often see Salvation Army bands playing music, such as **carols**, at Christmas time. While they play they may collect money from passers-by. The money is used to help people who are sick, hungry, or homeless.

17

CHRISTIAN ROCK AND FOLK MUSIC

Many Christians believe it is important to share their **faith** with as many people as possible. One way of doing this is by performing popular music, such as rock music, with a Christian message. They use electric guitars, electric bass guitars, keyboard instruments, drums and microphones just like any other rock band.

The musicians in this rock band share the Christian faith.

These musicians are playing folk music at a Christian service.

Many Christian worshippers enjoy informal folk music worship without a choir or organ. Often a group of singers with **acoustic** guitars will sing and play along with the worshippers. This kind of music can be performed in some churches, in halls, or in people's homes.

MUSIC AT HINDU CEREMONIES

Special occasions in the **Hindu** religion, such as weddings, will often have music. Different kinds of music can be used from **traditional** singing with instruments to Indian pop music and dancing. The music helps everyone to enjoy the ceremony.

This Hindu ceremony includes music.

violin

harmonium

flute

lute

voice

barrel drums

Any of these instruments can be used at a Hindu celebration.

There are many different instruments being used at this Hindu celebration, including barrel drums and an Indian lute. A barrel drum has a strap so it can be played with both hands. The Indian lute is a stringed instrument similar to a guitar.

TIBETAN TEMPLE MUSIC

Tibetan **Buddhism** is the main religion of Tibet and Mongolia. The monks who live in a Tibetan Buddhist temple are called lamas. Part of their worship is to **recite** Buddhist **scriptures** and **chant**. Tibetan chanting has a lot of low **notes**.

These Tibetan monks are performing in a Buddhist temple.

These Tibetan lamas are playing trumpets.

The lamas also play instruments which include trumpets and **percussion** instruments. Tibetan trumpets are made of metal. They can only play a few notes. They make a deep sound that can be heard far away.

JAPANESE TEMPLE MUSIC

The **traditional** religion of Japan is called Shinto. The religious music of Japan is called *kagura* which means "god music." The music is tradtionally performed to please the gods. New kagura music is still being written and performed in Japan.

These musicians are performing Japanese religious music.

These kagura musicians are playing a very large drum.

Kagura music includes singing and chanting. Drums, rattles, and flutes are also played. The music is performed in temples and also at festivals and special occasions. The big drums used in kagura music make a loud, pounding sound. The drummers often play them very gracefully, as if they were dancing as they play.

NEW ORLEANS FUNERAL MUSIC

The city of New Orleans in Louisiana is said to be the place where **jazz** music began. It was started by African-American people. In New Orleans there are sometimes **traditional** jazz funerals in which a jazz band walks with the funeral procession playing sad, slow music.

A traditional New Orleans funeral procession

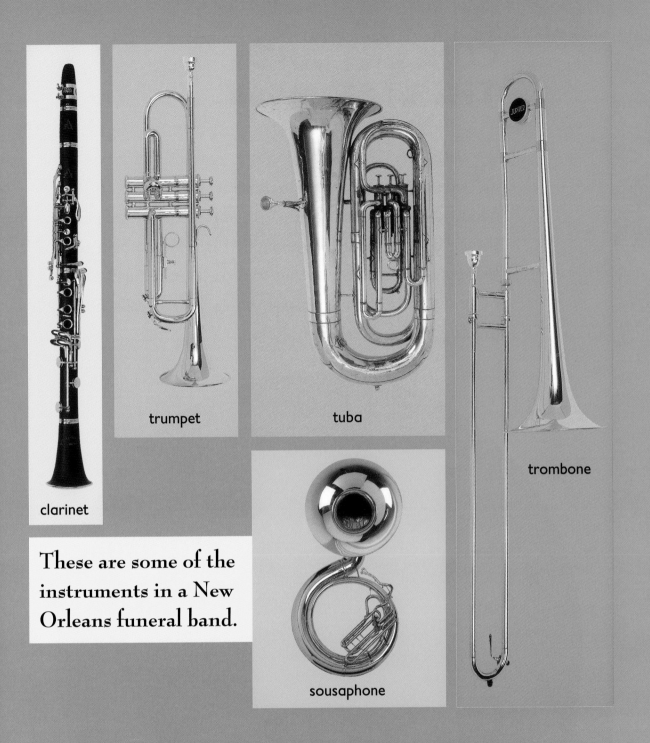

clarinet

trumpet

tuba

trombone

sousaphone

These are some of the instruments in a New Orleans funeral band.

The instruments the band play will usually include a clarinet, which is a **reed** instrument. There will also usually be a trumpet, a trombone, and a tuba or sousaphone, which are all **brass** instruments. These instruments are all used in jazz and marching band music as well.

CONCERT AND THEATER MUSIC

Some types of Christian music, such as oratorios, are performed in concert halls as well as in church. This is because many people enjoy listening to the music rather than it being an act of worship. An oratorio has a choir and **solo** singers. There can also be a classical orchestra of string, wind, and **percussion** instruments and an organ or other **keyboard** instruments.

This orchestra, choir, and solo singers are performing an oratorio.

This scene is from the stage musical
Jesus Christ Superstar.

There are several stage musicals based on religious stories. These mix pop and rock music with dancing and acting to tell the story. Many people enjoy them even if they do not share the religion in the story. The instruments used will often include electric guitars, keyboards, and drums as well as classical instruments. There will be solo singers for the important parts and often a chorus of extra singers as well.

GLOSSARY

acoustic instruments which do not have to be played through an electric amplifier

bellows an air-tight pouch which forces air into an instrument when it is squeezed

brass a type of hard metal used for making some wind instruments

Buddhism an Eastern religion

carols special Christian hymns and songs sung at Christmas

chant a type of singing used in many world religions. It is usually slow and uses only a small number of different notes

faith a set of religious beliefs. It can also mean the trust the believer places in them

Hindu someone who is a member of the Hindu faith, a religion which started in India

jazz a popular form of music started by African-Americans about one hundred years ago

keyboards electronic instruments played with keys like those of a piano or organ

missionaries people who travel to other countries to spread their religious faith

notes musical sounds

pedals levers on an instrument which are pressed by the player's feet

percussion instruments played by shaking or hitting

recite to sing or speak words from memory

reed thin strip of metal or cane which makes a sound when air is blown across it

religious orders groups of people who live together, often very simply, to concentrate on worship

rhythms the regular patterns of notes in music

sacred texts written teachings and rules which are important in a religion

scriptures written teachings and rules which are important in a religion

solo one musician singing or playing

tradition ways of doing things which have not changed for a long time

woodwind reed wind instruments such as the clarinet, saxophone, oboe, and flutes

MORE BOOKS TO READ

An older reader can help you with these books.

Durham, Montrew. *Mahalia Jackson: Young Gospel Singer.*
New York: Simon & Schuster. 1995.

Handel, George F., *Messiah: The Workbook for the Oratorio.*
New York: Harper Collins Children's Books. 1992.

INDEX